Balcony Women

Widow's Joy Journal

Balcony Women ™
Lifting Each Other Up In Love

"Therefore, encourage and build each other up."
1 Thessalonians 5:11

www.balconywomen.com

Balcony Women
Widow's Joy Journal

Published by Design Vault Press, LLC
www.designvaultpress.com

First Edition: May, 2022
ISBN: 978-1-7351818-4-4

What is a Balcony Woman?

A Balcony Woman is a woman God places in your life to encourage you. You will find her in the balcony of your life, hanging over the railing cheering you on. She is a woman who genuinely wants to see you succeed and is excited when good things happen to you.

Our nonprofit was formed to lift up, support and love the precious women in our communities. Proceeds from our online sales and nonprofit donations fund two widow dinners each year, host monthly widow support groups, furnish volunteer opportunities, provide encouragement and education, and fund small group curriculum for women of all ages with the goal of establishing supportive communities who will, in turn, fulfill God's calling to support the widows in their communities.

Learn more at www.balconywomen.com. Text "Balcony Women" to (202) 858-1233 or scan our code to donate.

*I*n the Bible, the feather represents care, love and protection.

Just as a bird soaring through the sky can view things from a higher perspective, the feather symbolizes the ability to see a bigger picture and understand what is important to focus on.

GOD.

"He will cover you with His feathers, and under His wings you will find refuge; His faithfulness will be your shield and rampart."
Psalms 91:4 (NIV)

Small Group Guide

While this Joy Journal is a useful tool on its own, it was designed to work hand-in-hand with our companion guide, "Balcony Women: An Inspirational Small Group Guide for Widows." The two were developed together to help widow groups of all sizes conduct their meetings, or help a widow on her grief journey when no widow support group is available. There is no directing, counseling, steering toward a predetermined goal, no manipulation, no "fixing" — just a complete reliance on God to work.

Our small group guide is divided into 12 sections, one for each monthly meeting. Each section has an opening prayer, widow voices, widow stories, Bible verses, a notes section, and a closing prayer. You're encouraged to use your Joy Journal in conjunction with the guide to help document your progress over time.

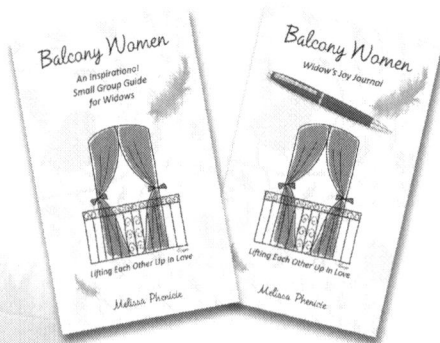

How to Use This Joy Journal

As mentioned earlier, this Joy Journal is a supplemental tool intended to be used in conjunction with our companion guide, "Balcony Women: An Inspirational Small Group Guide for Widows." The journal can be a useful outlet when you experience a grief trigger and are struggling. You can review your entries over time to see the progress you have made and be reminded of the God Sightings you've witnessed along your journey.

Using your Joy Journal is simple. Start by writing one positive thing that happens each day before you go to bed. It doesn't have to be a momentous event. It can be "I brushed my teeth today." The purpose of this tool is to focus on the good God is doing in your life. Start by listing one, then two, and gradually progressing to add more and more. Soon finding joyful moments becomes a positive habit. You will find yourself looking for the good in each day so that you will have content for your journal. We encourage you to journal Bible verses that speak to you, God Sightings you experience, as well as tools you have learned.

For additional inspiration, join our private Facebook page, @balconywomenforwidows.

__ / __ / __

List the positives:

1. _____

2. _____

3. _____

God Sightings/Bible Verse/ Grief Tools:

_____

_____

_____

_____

_____

_____

_____

_____

_____

– Joy Journal –

__ / __ / __

List the positives:

1. _____

2. _____

3. _____

God Sightings/Bible Verse/ Grief Tools:

_____

_____

_____

_____

_____

_____

_____

_____

_____

_____

___ / ___ / ___

List the positives:

1. _____

2. _____

3. _____

God Sightings/Bible Verse/ Grief Tools:

_____

_____

_____

_____

_____

_____

_____

_____

– Joy Journal –

__ / __ / __

List the positives:

1. _____

2. _____

3. _____

God Sightings/Bible Verse/ Grief Tools:

_____

_____

_____

_____

_____

_____

_____

_____

_____

_____

___ / ___ / ___

List the positives:

1. _____

2. _____

3. _____

God Sightings/Bible Verse/ Grief Tools:

_____

_____

_____

_____

_____

_____

_____

_____

_____

___ / ___ / ___

List the positives:

1. _____

2. _____

3. _____

God Sightings/Bible Verse/ Grief Tools:

_____

_____

_____

_____

_____

_____

_____

_____

_____

_____

__ / __ / __

List the positives:

1. _____

2. _____

3. _____

God Sightings/Bible Verse/ Grief Tools:

_____

_____

_____

_____

_____

_____

_____

_____

_____

– Joy Journal –

__ / __ / __

List the positives:

1. _____

2. _____

3. _____

God Sightings/Bible Verse/ Grief Tools:

_____

_____

_____

_____

_____

_____

_____

_____

_____

_____

__ / __ / __

List the positives:

1. _____

2. _____

3. _____

God Sightings/Bible Verse/ Grief Tools:

_____

_____

_____

_____

_____

_____

_____

_____

_____

__ / __ / __

List the positives:

1. _____

2. _____

3. _____

God Sightings/Bible Verse/ Grief Tools:

_____

_____

_____

_____

_____

_____

_____

_____

_____

__ / __ / __

List the positives:

1. _____

2. _____

3. _____

God Sightings/Bible Verse/ Grief Tools:

_____

_____

_____

_____

_____

_____

_____

_____

_____

__ / __ / __

List the positives:

1. _____

2. _____

3. _____

God Sightings/Bible Verse/ Grief Tools:

_____

_____

_____

_____

_____

_____

_____

_____

_____

__ / __ / __

List the positives:

1. _____

2. _____

3. _____

God Sightings/Bible Verse/ Grief Tools:

_____

_____

_____

_____

_____

_____

_____

_____

_____

– Joy Journal –

__ / __ / __

List the positives:

1. _____

2. _____

3. _____

God Sightings/Bible Verse/ Grief Tools:

_____

_____

_____

_____

_____

_____

_____

_____

_____

__ / __ / __

List the positives:

1. _____

2. _____

3. _____

God Sightings/Bible Verse/ Grief Tools:

_____

_____

_____

_____

_____

_____

_____

_____

_____

– Joy Journal –

__ / __ / __

List the positives:

1. _____

2. _____

3. _____

God Sightings/Bible Verse/ Grief Tools:

_____

_____

_____

_____

_____

_____

_____

_____

_____

_____

__ / __ / __

List the positives:

1. _____

2. _____

3. _____

God Sightings/Bible Verse/ Grief Tools:

_____

_____

_____

_____

_____

_____

_____

_____

_____

– Joy Journal –

__ / __ / __

List the positives:

1. _____

2. _____

3. _____

God Sightings/Bible Verse/ Grief Tools:

_____

_____

_____

_____

_____

_____

_____

_____

_____

__ / __ / __

List the positives:

1. _____

2. _____

3. _____

God Sightings/Bible Verse/ Grief Tools:

_____

_____

_____

_____

_____

_____

_____

_____

_____

_____

– Joy Journal –

__ / __ / __

List the positives:

1. _____

2. _____

3. _____

God Sightings/Bible Verse/ Grief Tools:

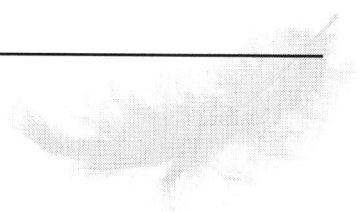

_____

_____

_____

_____

_____

_____

_____

_____

_____

_____

___ / ___ / ___

List the positives:

1. _____

2. _____

3. _____

God Sightings/Bible Verse/ Grief Tools:

_____

_____

_____

_____

_____

_____

_____

_____

_____

– Joy Journal –

___ /___ /___

List the positives:

1. _____

2. _____

3. _____

God Sightings/Bible Verse/ Grief Tools:

_____

_____

_____

_____

_____

_____

_____

_____

_____

__ / __ / __

List the positives:

1. _____

2. _____

3. _____

God Sightings/Bible Verse/ Grief Tools:

_____

_____

_____

_____

_____

_____

_____

_____

_____

– Joy Journal –

__ / __ / __

List the positives:

1. _____

2. _____

3. _____

God Sightings/Bible Verse/ Grief Tools:

_____

_____

_____

_____

_____

_____

_____

_____

_____

_____

__ / __ / __

List the positives:

1. _____

2. _____

3. _____

God Sightings/Bible Verse/ Grief Tools:

_____

_____

_____

_____

_____

_____

_____

_____

_____

_____

– Joy Journal –

__ / __ / __

List the positives:

1. _____

2. _____

3. _____

God Sightings/Bible Verse/ Grief Tools:

_____

_____

_____

_____

_____

_____

_____

_____

_____

___ / ___ / ___

List the positives:

1. _____

2. _____

3. _____

God Sightings/Bible Verse/ Grief Tools:

_____

_____

_____

_____

_____

_____

_____

_____

_____

_____

– Joy Journal –

__ / __ / __

List the positives:

1. _____

2. _____

3. _____

God Sightings/Bible Verse/ Grief Tools:

_____

_____

_____

_____

_____

_____

_____

_____

_____

__ / __ / __

List the positives:

1. _____

2. _____

3. _____

God Sightings/Bible Verse/ Grief Tools:

_____

_____

_____

_____

_____

_____

_____

_____

_____

– Joy Journal –

__ / __ / __

List the positives:

1. _____

2. _____

3. _____

God Sightings/Bible Verse/ Grief Tools:

_____

_____

_____

_____

_____

_____

_____

_____

_____

__ / __ / __

List the positives:

1. _____

2. _____

3. _____

God Sightings/Bible Verse/ Grief Tools:

_____

_____

_____

_____

_____

_____

_____

_____

_____

– Joy Journal –

___ / ___ / ___

List the positives:

1. _____

2. _____

3. _____

God Sightings/Bible Verse/ Grief Tools:

_____

_____

_____

_____

_____

_____

_____

_____

_____

_____

___ / ___ / ___

List the positives:

1. _____

2. _____

3. _____

God Sightings/Bible Verse/ Grief Tools:

_____

_____

_____

_____

_____

_____

_____

_____

_____

__ / __ / __

List the positives:

1. _____

2. _____

3. _____

God Sightings/Bible Verse/ Grief Tools:

_____

_____

_____

_____

_____

_____

_____

_____

_____

__ / __ / __

List the positives:

1. _____

2. _____

3. _____

God Sightings/Bible Verse/ Grief Tools:

_____

_____

_____

_____

_____

_____

_____

_____

_____

_____

___ / ___ / ___

List the positives:

1. _____

2. _____

3. _____

God Sightings/Bible Verse/ Grief Tools:

_____

_____

_____

_____

_____

_____

_____

_____

_____

_____

__ / __ / __

List the positives:

1. _____

2. _____

3. _____

God Sightings/Bible Verse/ Grief Tools:

_____

_____

_____

_____

_____

_____

_____

_____

_____

___ / ___ / ___

List the positives:

1. _____

2. _____

3. _____

God Sightings/Bible Verse/ Grief Tools:

_____

_____

_____

_____

_____

_____

_____

_____

_____

__ / __ / __

List the positives:

1. _____

2. _____

3. _____

God Sightings/Bible Verse/ Grief Tools:

_____

_____

_____

_____

_____

_____

_____

_____

– Joy Journal –

__ / __ / __

List the positives:

1. _____

2. _____

3. _____

God Sightings/Bible Verse/ Grief Tools:

_____

_____

_____

_____

_____

_____

_____

_____

_____

_____

__ / __ / __

List the positives:

1. _____

2. _____

3. _____

God Sightings/Bible Verse/ Grief Tools:

_____

_____

_____

_____

_____

_____

_____

_____

_____

___ / ___ / ___

List the positives:

1. _____

2. _____

3. _____

God Sightings/Bible Verse/ Grief Tools:

_____

_____

_____

_____

_____

_____

_____

_____

_____

__ / __ / __

List the positives:

1. _____

2. _____

3. _____

God Sightings/Bible Verse/ Grief Tools:

_____

_____

_____

_____

_____

_____

_____

_____

_____

– Joy Journal –

__ / __ / __

List the positives:

1. _____

2. _____

3. _____

God Sightings/Bible Verse/ Grief Tools:

_____

_____

_____

_____

_____

_____

_____

_____

_____

_____

__ / __ / __

List the positives:

1. _____

2. _____

3. _____

God Sightings/Bible Verse/ Grief Tools:

_____

_____

_____

_____

_____

_____

_____

_____

_____

– Joy Journal –

__ / __ / __

List the positives:

1. _____

2. _____

3. _____

God Sightings/Bible Verse/ Grief Tools:

_____

_____

_____

_____

_____

_____

_____

_____

_____

_____

__ / __ / __

List the positives:

1. _____

2. _____

3. _____

God Sightings/Bible Verse/ Grief Tools:

_____

_____

_____

_____

_____

_____

_____

_____

_____

– Joy Journal –

__ / __ / __

List the positives:

1. _____

2. _____

3. _____

God Sightings/Bible Verse/ Grief Tools:

_____

_____

_____

_____

_____

_____

_____

_____

_____

_____

__ / __ / __

List the positives:

1. _____

2. _____

3. _____

God Sightings/Bible Verse/ Grief Tools:

_____

_____

_____

_____

_____

_____

_____

_____

_____

_____

– Joy Journal –

___ / ___ / ___

List the positives:

1. _____

2. _____

3. _____

God Sightings/Bible Verse/ Grief Tools:

_____

_____

_____

_____

_____

_____

_____

_____

_____

_____

__ / __ / __

List the positives:

1. _____

2. _____

3. _____

God Sightings/Bible Verse/ Grief Tools:

_____

_____

_____

_____

_____

_____

_____

_____

_____

___ / ___ / ___

List the positives:

1. _____

2. _____

3. _____

God Sightings/Bible Verse/ Grief Tools:

_____

_____

_____

_____

_____

_____

_____

_____

_____

_____

__ / __ / __

List the positives:

1. _____

2. _____

3. _____

God Sightings/Bible Verse/ Grief Tools:

_____

_____

_____

_____

_____

_____

_____

_____

_____

– Joy Journal –

__ / __ / __

List the positives:

1. _____

2. _____

3. _____

God Sightings/Bible Verse/ Grief Tools:

_____

_____

_____

_____

_____

_____

_____

_____

_____

_____

__ / __ / __

List the positives:

1. _____

2. _____

3. _____

God Sightings/Bible Verse/ Grief Tools:

_____

_____

_____

_____

_____

_____

_____

_____

– Joy Journal –

___ / ___ / ___

List the positives:

1. _____

2. _____

3. _____

God Sightings/Bible Verse/ Grief Tools:

_____

_____

_____

_____

_____

_____

_____

_____

_____

_____

___ / ___ / ___

List the positives:

1. _____

2. _____

3. _____

God Sightings/Bible Verse/ Grief Tools:

_____

_____

_____

_____

_____

_____

_____

_____

_____

– Joy Journal –

__ / __ / __

List the positives:

1. _____

2. _____

3. _____

God Sightings/Bible Verse/ Grief Tools:

_____

_____

_____

_____

_____

_____

_____

_____

_____

__ / __ / __

List the positives:

1. _____

2. _____

3. _____

God Sightings/Bible Verse/ Grief Tools:

_____

_____

_____

_____

_____

_____

_____

_____

_____

_____

– Joy Journal –

__ / __ / __

List the positives:

1. _____

2. _____

3. _____

God Sightings/Bible Verse/ Grief Tools:

_____

_____

_____

_____

_____

_____

_____

_____

_____

_____

___ /___ /___

List the positives:

1. _____

2. _____

3. _____

God Sightings/Bible Verse/ Grief Tools:

_____

_____

_____

_____

_____

_____

_____

_____

– Joy Journal –

__ / __ / __

List the positives:

1. _____

2. _____

3. _____

God Sightings/Bible Verse/ Grief Tools:

_____

_____

_____

_____

_____

_____

_____

_____

_____

- Balcony Women -

__ / __ / __

List the positives:

1. _____

2. _____

3. _____

God Sightings/Bible Verse/ Grief Tools:

_____

_____

_____

_____

_____

_____

_____

_____

_____

– Joy Journal –

__ / __ / __

List the positives:

1. _____

2. _____

3. _____

God Sightings/Bible Verse/ Grief Tools:

_____

_____

_____

_____

_____

_____

_____

_____

_____

_____

__ / __ / __

List the positives:

1. _____

2. _____

3. _____

God Sightings/Bible Verse/ Grief Tools:

_____

_____

_____

_____

_____

_____

_____

_____

_____

_____

– Joy Journal –

__ / __ / __

List the positives:

1. _____

2. _____

3. _____

God Sightings/Bible Verse/ Grief Tools:

_____

_____

_____

_____

_____

_____

_____

_____

_____

__ / __ / __

List the positives:

1. _____

2. _____

3. _____

God Sightings/Bible Verse/ Grief Tools:

_____

_____

_____

_____

_____

_____

_____

_____

_____

_____

– Joy Journal –

___ / ___ / ___

List the positives:

1. _____

2. _____

3. _____

God Sightings/Bible Verse/ Grief Tools:

_____

_____

_____

_____

_____

_____

_____

_____

_____

__ / __ / __

List the positives:

1. _____

2. _____

3. _____

God Sightings/Bible Verse/ Grief Tools:

_____

_____

_____

_____

_____

_____

_____

_____

– Joy Journal –

__ / __ / __

List the positives:

1. _____

2. _____

3. _____

God Sightings/Bible Verse/ Grief Tools:

_____

_____

_____

_____

_____

_____

_____

_____

_____

_____

__ / __ / __

List the positives:

1. _____

2. _____

3. _____

God Sightings/Bible Verse/ Grief Tools:

_____

_____

_____

_____

_____

_____

_____

_____

_____

_____

– Joy Journal –

___ / ___ / ___

List the positives:

1. _____

2. _____

3. _____

God Sightings/Bible Verse/ Grief Tools:

_____

_____

_____

_____

_____

_____

_____

_____

_____

___ / ___ / ___

List the positives:

1. _____

2. _____

3. _____

God Sightings/Bible Verse/ Grief Tools:

_____

_____

_____

_____

_____

_____

_____

_____

_____

___ / ___ / ___

List the positives:

1. _____

2. _____

3. _____

God Sightings/Bible Verse/ Grief Tools:

_____

_____

_____

_____

_____

_____

_____

_____

_____

_____

___ / ___ / ___

List the positives:

1. _____

2. _____

3. _____

God Sightings/Bible Verse/ Grief Tools:

_____

_____

_____

_____

_____

_____

_____

_____

_____

– Joy Journal –

__ / __ / __

List the positives:

1. _____

2. _____

3. _____

God Sightings/Bible Verse/ Grief Tools:

_____

_____

_____

_____

_____

_____

_____

_____

_____

_____

__ / __ / __

List the positives:

1. _____

2. _____

3. _____

God Sightings/Bible Verse/ Grief Tools:

_____

_____

_____

_____

_____

_____

_____

_____

_____

_____

– Joy Journal –

__ / __ / __

List the positives:

1. _____

2. _____

3. _____

God Sightings/Bible Verse/ Grief Tools:

_____

_____

_____

_____

_____

_____

_____

_____

_____

_____

__ / __ / __

List the positives:

1. _____

2. _____

3. _____

God Sightings/Bible Verse/ Grief Tools:

_____

_____

_____

_____

_____

_____

_____

_____

_____

_____

– Joy Journal –

__ / __ / __

List the positives:

1. _____

2. _____

3. _____

God Sightings/Bible Verse/ Grief Tools:

_____

_____

_____

_____

_____

_____

_____

_____

_____

__ / __ / __

List the positives:

1. _____

2. _____

3. _____

God Sightings/Bible Verse/ Grief Tools:

_____

_____

_____

_____

_____

_____

_____

_____

_____

– Joy Journal –

__ / __ / __

List the positives:

1. _____

2. _____

3. _____

God Sightings/Bible Verse/ Grief Tools:

_____

_____

_____

_____

_____

_____

_____

_____

_____

__ / __ / __

List the positives:

1. _____

2. _____

3. _____

God Sightings/Bible Verse/ Grief Tools:

_____

_____

_____

_____

_____

_____

_____

_____

_____

_____

– Joy Journal –

___ / ___ / ___

List the positives:

1. _____

2. _____

3. _____

God Sightings/Bible Verse/ Grief Tools:

_____

_____

_____

_____

_____

_____

_____

_____

_____

__ / __ / __

List the positives:

1. _____

2. _____

3. _____

God Sightings/Bible Verse/ Grief Tools:

_____

_____

_____

_____

_____

_____

_____

_____

_____

– Joy Journal –

__ / __ / __

List the positives:

1. _____

2. _____

3. _____

God Sightings/Bible Verse/ Grief Tools:

_____

_____

_____

_____

_____

_____

_____

_____

_____

_____

__ / __ / __

List the positives:

1. _____

2. _____

3. _____

God Sightings/Bible Verse/ Grief Tools:

_____

_____

_____

_____

_____

_____

_____

_____

_____

_____

– Joy Journal –

__ / __ / __

List the positives:

1. _____

2. _____

3. _____

God Sightings/Bible Verse/ Grief Tools:

_____

_____

_____

_____

_____

_____

_____

_____

_____

__ / __ / __

List the positives:

1. _____

2. _____

3. _____

God Sightings/Bible Verse/ Grief Tools:

_____

_____

_____

_____

_____

_____

_____

_____

_____

– Joy Journal –

__ / __ / __

List the positives:

1. _____

2. _____

3. _____

God Sightings/Bible Verse/ Grief Tools:

_____

_____

_____

_____

_____

_____

_____

_____

_____

__ / __ / __

List the positives:

1. _____

2. _____

3. _____

God Sightings/Bible Verse/ Grief Tools:

_____

_____

_____

_____

_____

_____

_____

_____

_____

_____

– Joy Journal –

___ / ___ / ___

List the positives:

1. _____

2. _____

3. _____

God Sightings/Bible Verse/ Grief Tools:

_____

_____

_____

_____

_____

_____

_____

_____

_____

___ / ___ / ___

List the positives:

1. _____

2. _____

3. _____

God Sightings/Bible Verse/ Grief Tools:

_____

_____

_____

_____

_____

_____

_____

_____

_____

– Joy Journal –

__ / __ / __

List the positives:

1. _____

2. _____

3. _____

God Sightings/Bible Verse/ Grief Tools:

_____

_____

_____

_____

_____

_____

_____

_____

_____

_____

__ / __ / __

List the positives:

1. _____

2. _____

3. _____

God Sightings/Bible Verse/ Grief Tools:

_____

_____

_____

_____

_____

_____

_____

_____

_____

_____

– Joy Journal –

___ / ___ / ___

List the positives:

1. _____

2. _____

3. _____

God Sightings/Bible Verse/ Grief Tools:

_____

_____

_____

_____

_____

_____

_____

_____

_____

__ / __ / __

List the positives:

1. _____

2. _____

3. _____

God Sightings/Bible Verse/ Grief Tools:

_____

_____

_____

_____

_____

_____

_____

_____

_____

– Joy Journal –

__ / __ / __

List the positives:

1. _____

2. _____

3. _____

God Sightings/Bible Verse/ Grief Tools:

_____

_____

_____

_____

_____

_____

_____

_____

_____

__ / __ / __

List the positives:

1. _____

2. _____

3. _____

God Sightings/Bible Verse/ Grief Tools:

_____

_____

_____

_____

_____

_____

_____

_____

_____

_____

– Joy Journal –

__ / __ / __

List the positives:

1. _____

2. _____

3. _____

God Sightings/Bible Verse/ Grief Tools:

_____

_____

_____

_____

_____

_____

_____

_____

_____

_____

__ / __ / __

List the positives:

1. _____

2. _____

3. _____

God Sightings/Bible Verse/ Grief Tools:

_____

_____

_____

_____

_____

_____

_____

_____

_____

– Joy Journal –

__ / __ / __

List the positives:

1. _____

2. _____

3. _____

God Sightings/Bible Verse/ Grief Tools:

_____

_____

_____

_____

_____

_____

_____

_____

_____

__ / __ / __

List the positives:

1. _____

2. _____

3. _____

God Sightings/Bible Verse/ Grief Tools:

_____

_____

_____

_____

_____

_____

_____

_____

– Joy Journal –

___ / ___ / ___

List the positives:

1. _____

2. _____

3. _____

God Sightings/Bible Verse/ Grief Tools:

_____

_____

_____

_____

_____

_____

_____

_____

_____

_____

__ / __ / __

List the positives:

1. _____

2. _____

3. _____

God Sightings/Bible Verse/ Grief Tools:

_____

_____

_____

_____

_____

_____

_____

_____

_____

– Joy Journal –

__ / __ / __

List the positives:

1. _____

2. _____

3. _____

God Sightings/Bible Verse/ Grief Tools:

_____

_____

_____

_____

_____

_____

_____

_____

_____

_____

__ / __ / __

List the positives:

1. _____

2. _____

3. _____

God Sightings/Bible Verse/ Grief Tools:

_____

_____

_____

_____

_____

_____

_____

_____

_____

– Joy Journal –

__ / __ / __

List the positives:

1. _____

2. _____

3. _____

God Sightings/Bible Verse/ Grief Tools:

_____

_____

_____

_____

_____

_____

_____

_____

_____

_____

__ / __ / __

List the positives:

1. _____

2. _____

3. _____

God Sightings/Bible Verse/ Grief Tools:

_____

_____

_____

_____

_____

_____

_____

_____

_____

___ / ___ / ___

List the positives:

1. _____

2. _____

3. _____

God Sightings/Bible Verse/ Grief Tools:

_____

_____

_____

_____

_____

_____

_____

_____

_____

__ / __ / __

List the positives:

1. _____

2. _____

3. _____

God Sightings/Bible Verse/ Grief Tools:

_____

_____

_____

_____

_____

_____

_____

_____

_____

– Joy Journal –

__ / __ / __

List the positives:

1. _____

2. _____

3. _____

God Sightings/Bible Verse/ Grief Tools:

_____

_____

_____

_____

_____

_____

_____

_____

_____

_____

__ / __ / __

List the positives:

1. _____

2. _____

3. _____

God Sightings/Bible Verse/ Grief Tools:

_____

_____

_____

_____

_____

_____

_____

_____

_____

– Joy Journal –

___ / ___ / ___

List the positives:

1. _____

2. _____

3. _____

God Sightings/Bible Verse/ Grief Tools:

_____

_____

_____

_____

_____

_____

_____

_____

_____

__ / __ / __

List the positives:

1. _____

2. _____

3. _____

God Sightings/Bible Verse/ Grief Tools:

_____

_____

_____

_____

_____

_____

_____

_____

_____

_____

– Joy Journal –

__ / __ / __

List the positives:

1. _____

2. _____

3. _____

God Sightings/Bible Verse/ Grief Tools:

_____

_____

_____

_____

_____

_____

_____

_____

_____

_____

__ / __ / __

List the positives:

1. _____

2. _____

3. _____

God Sightings/Bible Verse/ Grief Tools:

_____

_____

_____

_____

_____

_____

_____

_____

_____

_____

___ / ___ / ___

List the positives:

1. _____

2. _____

3. _____

God Sightings/Bible Verse/ Grief Tools:

_____

_____

_____

_____

_____

_____

_____

_____

_____

_____

___ /___ /___

List the positives:

1. _____

2. _____

3. _____

God Sightings/Bible Verse/ Grief Tools:

_____

_____

_____

_____

_____

_____

_____

_____

_____

___ / ___ / ___

List the positives:

1. _____

2. _____

3. _____

God Sightings/Bible Verse/ Grief Tools:

_____

_____

_____

_____

_____

_____

_____

_____

_____

__ / __ / __

List the positives:

1. _____

2. _____

3. _____

God Sightings/Bible Verse/ Grief Tools:

_____

_____

_____

_____

_____

_____

_____

_____

_____

– Joy Journal –

__ / __ / __

List the positives:

1. _____

2. _____

3. _____

God Sightings/Bible Verse/ Grief Tools:

_____

_____

_____

_____

_____

_____

_____

_____

_____

__ / __ / __

List the positives:

1. _____

2. _____

3. _____

God Sightings/Bible Verse/ Grief Tools:

_____

_____

_____

_____

_____

_____

_____

_____

_____

_____

– Joy Journal –

__ / __ / __

List the positives:

1. _____

2. _____

3. _____

God Sightings/Bible Verse/ Grief Tools:

_____

_____

_____

_____

_____

_____

_____

_____

_____

_____

___ / ___ / ___

List the positives:

1. _____

2. _____

3. _____

God Sightings/Bible Verse/ Grief Tools:

_____

_____

_____

_____

_____

_____

_____

_____

_____

– Joy Journal –

__ / __ / __

List the positives:

1. _____

2. _____

3. _____

God Sightings/Bible Verse/ Grief Tools:

_____

_____

_____

_____

_____

_____

_____

_____

_____

_____

__ / __ / __

List the positives:

1. _____

2. _____

3. _____

God Sightings/Bible Verse/ Grief Tools:

_____

_____

_____

_____

_____

_____

_____

_____

_____

_____

– Joy Journal –

___ / ___ / ___

List the positives:

1. _____

2. _____

3. _____

God Sightings/Bible Verse/ Grief Tools:

_____

_____

_____

_____

_____

_____

_____

_____

_____

__ / __ / __

List the positives:

1. _____

2. _____

3. _____

God Sightings/Bible Verse/ Grief Tools:

_____

_____

_____

_____

_____

_____

_____

_____

_____

__ / __ / __

List the positives:

1. _____

2. _____

3. _____

God Sightings/Bible Verse/ Grief Tools:

_____

_____

_____

_____

_____

_____

_____

_____

_____

___ / ___ / ___

List the positives:

1. _____

2. _____

3. _____

God Sightings/Bible Verse/ Grief Tools:

_____

_____

_____

_____

_____

_____

_____

_____

– Joy Journal –

___ / ___ / ___

List the positives:

1. _____

2. _____

3. _____

God Sightings/Bible Verse/ Grief Tools:

_____

_____

_____

_____

_____

_____

_____

_____

_____

_____

___ / ___ / ___

List the positives:

1. _____

2. _____

3. _____

God Sightings/Bible Verse/ Grief Tools:

_____

_____

_____

_____

_____

_____

_____

_____

_____

– Joy Journal –

__ / __ / __

List the positives:

1. _____

2. _____

3. _____

God Sightings/Bible Verse/ Grief Tools:

_____

_____

_____

_____

_____

_____

_____

_____

_____

_____

__ / __ / __

List the positives:

1. _____

2. _____

3. _____

God Sightings/Bible Verse/ Grief Tools:

_____

_____

_____

_____

_____

_____

_____

_____

_____

— Joy Journal —

__ / __ / __

List the positives:

1. _____

2. _____

3. _____

God Sightings/Bible Verse/ Grief Tools:

_____

_____

_____

_____

_____

_____

_____

_____

_____

___ / ___ / ___

List the positives:

1. _____

2. _____

3. _____

God Sightings/Bible Verse/ Grief Tools:

_____

_____

_____

_____

_____

_____

_____

_____

_____

_____

– Joy Journal –

__ / __ / __

List the positives:

1. _____

2. _____

3. _____

God Sightings/Bible Verse/ Grief Tools:

_____

_____

_____

_____

_____

_____

_____

_____

_____

__ / __ / __

List the positives:

1. _____

2. _____

3. _____

God Sightings/Bible Verse/ Grief Tools:

_____

_____

_____

_____

_____

_____

_____

_____

_____

– Joy Journal –

___ / ___ / ___

List the positives:

1. _____

2. _____

3. _____

God Sightings/Bible Verse/ Grief Tools:

_____

_____

_____

_____

_____

_____

_____

_____

_____

_____

__ / __ / __

List the positives:

1. _____

2. _____

3. _____

God Sightings/Bible Verse/ Grief Tools:

_____

_____

_____

_____

_____

_____

_____

_____

_____

_____

– Joy Journal –

__ / __ / __

List the positives:

1. _____

2. _____

3. _____

God Sightings/Bible Verse/ Grief Tools:

_____

_____

_____

_____

_____

_____

_____

_____

_____

_____

__ / __ / __

List the positives:

1. _____

2. _____

3. _____

God Sightings/Bible Verse/ Grief Tools:

_____

_____

_____

_____

_____

_____

_____

_____

_____

– Joy Journal –

___ / ___ / ___

List the positives:

1. _____

2. _____

3. _____

God Sightings/Bible Verse/ Grief Tools:

_____

_____

_____

_____

_____

_____

_____

_____

_____

_____

__ / __ / __

List the positives:

1. _____

2. _____

3. _____

God Sightings/Bible Verse/ Grief Tools:

_____

_____

_____

_____

_____

_____

_____

_____

_____

– Joy Journal –

__ / __ / __

List the positives:

1. _____

2. _____

3. _____

God Sightings/Bible Verse/ Grief Tools:

_____

_____

_____

_____

_____

_____

_____

_____

_____

_____

___ / ___ / ___

List the positives:

1. _____

2. _____

3. _____

God Sightings/Bible Verse/ Grief Tools:

_____

_____

_____

_____

_____

_____

_____

_____

_____

_____

– Joy Journal –

__ / __ / __

List the positives:

1. _____

2. _____

3. _____

God Sightings/Bible Verse/ Grief Tools:

_____

_____

_____

_____

_____

_____

_____

_____

_____

_____

__ / __ / __

List the positives:

1. _____

2. _____

3. _____

God Sightings/Bible Verse/ Grief Tools:

_____

_____

_____

_____

_____

_____

_____

_____

_____

– Joy Journal –

__ / __ / __

List the positives:

1. _____

2. _____

3. _____

God Sightings/Bible Verse/ Grief Tools:

_____

_____

_____

_____

_____

_____

_____

_____

_____

__ / __ / __

List the positives:

1. _____

2. _____

3. _____

God Sightings/Bible Verse/ Grief Tools:

_____

_____

_____

_____

_____

_____

_____

_____

_____

– Joy Journal –

__ / __ / __

List the positives:

1. _____

2. _____

3. _____

God Sightings/Bible Verse/ Grief Tools:

_____

_____

_____

_____

_____

_____

_____

_____

_____

__ / __ / __

List the positives:

1. _____

2. _____

3. _____

God Sightings/Bible Verse/ Grief Tools:

_____

_____

_____

_____

_____

_____

_____

_____

_____

– Joy Journal –

__ / __ / __

List the positives:

1. _____

2. _____

3. _____

God Sightings/Bible Verse/ Grief Tools:

_____

_____

_____

_____

_____

_____

_____

_____

_____

_____

___ / ___ / ___

List the positives:

1. _____

2. _____

3. _____

God Sightings/Bible Verse/ Grief Tools:

_____

_____

_____

_____

_____

_____

_____

_____

_____

_____

– Joy Journal –

__ / __ / __

List the positives:

1. _____

2. _____

3. _____

God Sightings/Bible Verse/ Grief Tools:

_____

_____

_____

_____

_____

_____

_____

_____

_____

_____

__ / __ / __

List the positives:

1. _____

2. _____

3. _____

God Sightings/Bible Verse/ Grief Tools:

_____

_____

_____

_____

_____

_____

_____

_____

_____

__ / __ / __

List the positives:

1. _____

2. _____

3. _____

God Sightings/Bible Verse/ Grief Tools:

_____

_____

_____

_____

_____

_____

_____

_____

_____

___ / ___ / ___

List the positives:

1. _____

2. _____

3. _____

God Sightings/Bible Verse/ Grief Tools:

_____

_____

_____

_____

_____

_____

_____

_____

_____

__ / __ / __

List the positives:

1. _____

2. _____

3. _____

God Sightings/Bible Verse/ Grief Tools:

_____

_____

_____

_____

_____

_____

_____

_____

_____

- Balcony Women -

__ / __ / __

List the positives:

1. _____

2. _____

3. _____

God Sightings/Bible Verse/ Grief Tools:

_____

_____

_____

_____

_____

_____

_____

_____

_____

__ / __ / __

List the positives:

1. _____

2. _____

3. _____

God Sightings/Bible Verse/ Grief Tools:

_____

_____

_____

_____

_____

_____

_____

_____

_____

_____

___ / ___ / ___

List the positives:

1. _____

2. _____

3. _____

God Sightings/Bible Verse/ Grief Tools:

_____

_____

_____

_____

_____

_____

_____

_____

_____

__ / __ / __

List the positives:

1. _____

2. _____

3. _____

God Sightings/Bible Verse/ Grief Tools:

_____

_____

_____

_____

_____

_____

_____

_____

_____

_____

___ / ___ / ___

List the positives:

1. _____

2. _____

3. _____

God Sightings/Bible Verse/ Grief Tools:

_____

_____

_____

_____

_____

_____

_____

_____

_____

_____

– Joy Journal –

__ / __ / __

List the positives:

1. _____

2. _____

3. _____

God Sightings/Bible Verse/ Grief Tools:

_____

_____

_____

_____

_____

_____

_____

_____

_____

_____

__ / __ / __

List the positives:

1. _____

2. _____

3. _____

God Sightings/Bible Verse/ Grief Tools:

_____

_____

_____

_____

_____

_____

_____

_____

_____

_____

– Joy Journal –

__ / __ / __

List the positives:

1. _____

2. _____

3. _____

God Sightings/Bible Verse/ Grief Tools:

_____

_____

_____

_____

_____

_____

_____

_____

_____

_____

__ / __ / __

List the positives:

1. _____

2. _____

3. _____

God Sightings/Bible Verse/ Grief Tools:

_____

_____

_____

_____

_____

_____

_____

_____

_____

– Joy Journal –

__ / __ / __

List the positives:

1. _____

2. _____

3. _____

God Sightings/Bible Verse/ Grief Tools:

_____

_____

_____

_____

_____

_____

_____

_____

_____

__ / __ / __

List the positives:

1. _____

2. _____

3. _____

God Sightings/Bible Verse/ Grief Tools:

_____

_____

_____

_____

_____

_____

_____

_____

_____

– Joy Journal –

__ / __ / __

List the positives:

1. _____

2. _____

3. _____

God Sightings/Bible Verse/ Grief Tools:

_____

_____

_____

_____

_____

_____

_____

_____

_____

__ / __ / __

List the positives:

1. _____

2. _____

3. _____

God Sightings/Bible Verse/ Grief Tools:

_____

_____

_____

_____

_____

_____

_____

_____

_____

_____

___ / ___ / ___

List the positives:

1. _____

2. _____

3. _____

God Sightings/Bible Verse/ Grief Tools:

_____

_____

_____

_____

_____

_____

_____

_____

_____

_____

To learn more about Balcony Women,
visit www.balconywomen.com.

Balcony Women
Lifting Each Other Up In Love

Bringing new adventures to life, one word at a time.

DesignVault
PRESS

www.designvaultpress.com

Made in the USA
Columbia, SC
19 June 2022